HUMAN NATURE,

THE STERLING,

THE FALLACIOUS,

AND THE HIDEOUS

HUMAN NATURE,

THE STERLING,
THE FALLACIOUS,
AND THE HIDEOUS

Salvador DeLaRosa

Library of Congress Control Number: 2017902962
ISBN: Hardcover 978-1-5245-8520-4
Softcover 978-1-5245-8519-8
eBook 978-1-5245-8518-1

Print information available on the last page.

Rev. date: 03/10/2017

To order additional copies of this book, contact:
Xlibris
1-888-795-4274
www.Xlibris.com
Orders@Xlibris.com
753869

Contents

Acknowledgment

Three worthy fans I want to write a word of appreciation for their support and comments which helped with the writing of this book.
Gratitude to my wife Iryna De La Rosa, my
brother Guillermo De La Rosa,
and a special recognition to my friend Edward
J. Kruck, from the beginning
to the final manuscript our conversations
encouraged and inspired me with
absolute conviction that publishing a compilation
of poetic articles, cultural,
and political poems was achievable.

Who would guess workouts at the gym would not only challenge the body but the mind as well? Through thought provoking conversations and more light hearted banter, I was privileged to hear first- hand the author's works and honored that he requested my opinion on each one. I hope the reader appreciates and enjoys the author's skill and wit as I did in assembling these fine works of poetry.

Edward J. Kruck

The Color Of Suits

Traditional, contemporary, modern till this day are distinguished by complexion

The fiber deeply embedded is the undeniable dissimilarity amongst all

Complexion has at times interchanged when a quarrel alters the balance of an era

But the fiber immersed: after concretely crystallized will never transmogrify

Justifying the value of tellurians unequivocally through the view of iridescence is ignominious..

I was inspired to write The Color Of Suits after viewing Barack Obama hugging Hillary Clinton on the July 28th, 2016 Democratic Convention.

An inspiration of opportunity, two extremely powerful figures authenticating to the World that unity purges all impediments to overcome any type of social concern.

A Cent Or Less
A Sense Or Less

Rate of valuation of a spurious kinsperson is ultimately
determined in the realm of negative numbers, hopefully
above the ten foot realm

Sentient entities have obliterated ecological niches without a
cent of pity

Rationalization, hardly; encouragement for continuance is far
more acceptable

Mellifluous living sounds prohibitive, but freely obtainable
one sense at a time

Allocating immense value to ludicrous non essentials causing
a grave diversion of what really matters: US

Change, Is It Authentic Or Imaginary?

Is it possible for the World to change while human nature is at an impasse?

A bold statement to say, adjustments is the change that never occurs

For the sake of simplicity, simple short term adjustments followed by abstract long term advancements carried over through generations proclaiming an alleged effect that change has taken place

Genuine metamorphosis of human nature would beg the argument, why does history continue to repeat itself, we are responsible for repeating it.

Even with the vast enhancements in technology, we continue to falter upon the same mistakes since the beginning of time as we know it

The Elected Garden

It's demands are negligible in comparison to so many
extracted gifts destroying its sublime beauty

Imperious we are, to displace tenancy of any creature that
disrupts our future possessions

As the engraved thought of ownership has corrupted proper
definition of earth's viability as a living organism(prediction
of the Gaia hypothesis), continuance to full destruction is
inevitable

Will we know whom to mourn on such a day, our destruction
or Earth's

A Dickensian World Equals Social Divergence

A human balancing the scale of virtues at it's epicenter is a rare breed indeed, a single unitary valorous action and a warranted entitlement to Knighthood and titled a munificent being is assured to proceed

"In 1914, Henry Ford doubled his workers' pay from $2.34 to $5 a day, recognizing that paying people more would enable them to afford the cars they were producing. Reduction of income levels and employment security ultimately reduces consumption and economic activity, impoverishing most within societies."

A sheer one hundred & two years later: On April 13, 2016" Dan Price, the young chief executive officer of Gravity Payments, a Seattle-based credit card processing company, told his staff he was raising their minimum salary to $70,000 a year. Some employees would see their wages double. There was more: He planned to cut his own $1.1million compensation to help cover the cost."

As all others melee to justify their breed with think tank studies and sacrificial cost with well decorated excuses, as Social Inequality continues to widen.

An irrepressible disproportionate gap treasured by our current and alleged Sharing Economy

Diplomacy

Thought by the masses as a laborious surefire method in circumventing grave controversy

Hindsight has proliferated throughout history that the masses have advocated diplomacy as the legitimate resolution in avoiding bloodshed

The acrid truth is its ambiguity exists & is denying the peace we are all yearning for...

Medieval times, the pair involved the Church & King, one used the almighty for its purposeful sacrificial offers, the King simply used power for all his sacrificial offers

Separation of State & Church with a diplomatic agreement of absolute tax exemption

Behemoth institutions laboring together for our benefit, the Church very skillful in the art of mind purification guaranteed votes in exchange for (?)

Institutions today are disguising themselves by offering rain drops of hope to the masses, when in reality change has never happened, it has been adjusted.

We are at the maximal point of ***GREED & SELF INTEREST.***

Greed without rein is synonymous with perverted Power

Self interest without rein is synonymous with the carnage of mother nature

An uninterrupted, boundless, unwavering, steadfast, self perpetuating vicious cycle without any deterrent or hindrance to slow its path...

Grandis Bellus Inne Aefre aelcYnce

The scenography before us is immensely sublime and
resplendently magnificent

A grandeur transcendent sphere encompassing all
seven beauties "Extravagant,Transgressive, Emergent,
Transformative, Ethereal, Intricate, and Elemental"

Every encountered visual instance will sojourn your soul
to a hypnotic event exemplifying all seven with contrasting
elevation of beauty horripilating through your being one by one

Ego Multum Mirari

Is it thinkable, the media is at the service of a dominant elite culture?

As we are in a dire urgency of responsible information from our journalist, seems there are two standards, one which is filtered and re-filtered to purposefully contradict reality, the second one concealed in a vacuum of despair until time, ashes its validity

A merited clarification of their respectful duty to conduct their vocation with a preeminent sense of ethics, averting, beyond all calling to divert the truth from the public

The Emancipating Of The Mind & Conscious

Living severely ambushed by hidden common interest can lead to a life of infelicity

Common interest are natural and cannot be ignored by all or anyone

Balancing, tweaking, and suppressing them at times of distress can lead to life of kinship with everyone who surrounds us.

The seventh sense, not to be confused with the superego (Sigmund Freud) or the sixth sense (perception), a judge outside the realm of our natural interests that when called upon will objectively draw a conclusion

Extrinsic Shadows

Intrinsic shadows are genuinely recognizable as we own it from childbirth

Self preservation will defend it from harming itself or harm by another

To protect its stature from nullification it will embark on a quest of protectionism

Without regard for the number of extrinsic shadows it amasses for their final day

Flawed planning in essence, it is not an indecipherable riddle, the fact that every instance of protectionism is not a final resolution for the upkeep of stature, but temporary resolves that will continue with every threat that attempts to disannul position of prominence or to secure future enhancements of thy name

Cognizance of the flaw, be that as it may an insurance stratagem to secure the Chinese Divine Pantheon of the three monkeys

"HEAR NO EVIL, SEE NO EVIL, SPEAK NO EVIL"

Fictional – Nonfictional You Conclude

Bank of America: There's a 20%-50% chance we're inside the matrix and reality is just a simulation, based on Nick Bostrom seminal paper.

After digesting the headline I could not resist a Jokers' Wild grin embellished with irony

Calling on all savers to sprint over to Bank Of Americas' locations and open a virtual account and profit with real money

What a belated eccentric headline referenced & posted by a bank, they've just discovered the yellow brick road to Kansas

George Orwell's 1984 dystopian novel is a fictional and rudimentary beginnings of the matrix, lets not dismiss from mind this is 1984

A prerequisite read for those who are inspirited to the fact that this novel was fiction in hindsight, but today its a dystopian nonfictional novel of the matrix

1984; fear, torture & brainwashing were the tools utilized to control the population

March 31, 1999 in the matrix trilogy hard wiring was the tool used for the same intendment

21st century wireless devices is the tool used for the same intendment

The matrix is not real as a virtual simulation because we have never left the matrix

That the matrix environment changes in accordance with the available tools at the present time & place is quite obvious, what never changes is its intentions to control the human mind in order to achieve behavior that satisfies the top brass

The next matrix environment is already underway

For decades, DARPA, the secretive research arm of the Department of Defense, has dreamed of turning soldiers into cyborgs. And now it's finally happening. The agency has funded projects that involve implanting chips into soldiers' brains that could one day enhance performance on the battlefield and repair traumatized brains once the fog of war has lifted. "Of the 2.5 million Americans who served in Iraq and Afghanistan, 300,000 of them came home with traumatic brain injury," journalist Annie Jacobsentold NPR. "DARPA initiated a series of programs to help cognitive functioning, to repair some of this damage. And those programs center around putting brain chips inside the tissue of the brain."

In her new book about the history of DARPA, "The Pentagon's Brain," Jacobsen writes about DARPA's "classified brain programs." Scientists, she says, are already testing "implantable wireless 'neuroprosthetics'" to help soldiers with brain injuries. "[S]oldiers allow the tiny machines, or chips, to be implanted in their brain," Jacobsen writes in the book. "Despite multiple appeals through the Office of the Secretary of Defense, DARPA declined to grant me an interview with any of these brain-wounded warriors." A DARPA spokesperson told Fusion that "brain-neural interfaces" have not been implanted in soldiers, though researchers have already begun testing such devices by temporarily implanting electrical arrays into the brains of volunteers undergoing surgery for other neurological issues. Defense One,an online magazine that covers the military, reported last year on

DARPA's work on brain chips to treat PTSD, and said that DARPA was not yet in the testing phase. When DARPA launched its RAM (Restoring Active Memory) program last year, it projected it would be about four years until researchers were implanting permanent chips in humans.

Creating super soldiers isn't the only thing that DARPA is trying to do, Jacobsen says. According to her new book, published by Little, Brown, government scientists hope that implanting chips in soldiers will unlock the secrets of artificial intelligence, and allow us to give machines the kind of higher-level reasoning that humans can do.

"When you see all of these brain mapping programs going on, many scientists wonder whether this will [be what it takes] to break that long-sought barrier of AI," said Jacobsen in a phosne interview.

For Jacobsen, who has spent her career chronicling war, weapons and U.S. government secrets, digging through DARPA documents provided a glimpse at the future of war, but also raised questions about whether that future is one we really want.

"Are hunter-killer robots right around the bend?" she writes in the book..

Since the collapse of the Soviet Union in the 1990s, the Defense Advanced Research Projects Agency has poured resources into far-out research, from solving infectious disease to transforming humans for the theater of war. The agency is pioneering Iron Man-like exoskeletons to help protect soldiers from fire and the elements so they can keep fighting for longer. And under initiatives like the Brain-Machine Interface, defense scientists have studied how brain implants could eventually enhance a soldier's cognition. The brain emits electrical signals and an implanted chip can tap into those signals to read them. Outside of the government, scientists at places like Berkeley's Brain-Machine Interface Systems Laboratory are experimenting with how to use such implants to translate thoughts into action for people with neurological impairments, eventually hoping to, for example, help a paralyzed person move.

At DARPA, programs like RAM and REMIND (Restorative Encoding Memory Integration Neural Device)have explored how brain implants might help soldiers returning from war with traumatic brain injuries impacting memory. Other DARPA programs have envisioned allowing soldiers at battle to communicate by thought alone.

"Imagine a time when the human brain has its own wireless modem so that instead of acting on thoughts, war fighters have thoughts that act," Jacobsen recounts DARPA's Eric Eisenstadt telling a crowd at a technology conference in 2002.

But Jacobsen's warning is that while helping soldiers suffering in the aftermath of war may seem inherently benign, we must not forget that DARPA is in the business of defense. The question that should punctuate everything DARPA does, Jacobsen suggests, is "How can this be weaponized?"

DARPA's spokesperson told Fusion that the main goal of its brain-related work is not offensive military applications, but to develop therapeutic devices for soldiers and veterans.

"Suggesting that we aim to develop 'super soldiers' or that our brain-related research is being conducted to 'unlock the secrets of artificial intelligence' is patently false,'" he said.

Understanding the human brain is as important to achieving artificial intelligence as understanding computers. "The Pentagon is clearly very confident that they're moving toward autonomous weapons," Jacobsen told me. "The question is where is that confidence coming from?"

*We've updated the headline to make it clearer to reflect comments from DARPA. The story is based on an interview with journalist Annie Jacobsen, who wrote a new book on the history of DARPA, but who does not name sources when reporting on chips implanted in soldiers' brains. After publication, we added quotes from DARPA saying that it will be several years before chips are ready to be permanently implanted in soldiers.

I'll take a wild guess on what will be the next matrix environment to follow:

Phase1= ***Universal Soldiers Cyborg Soldiers***

Phase 2 = ***Judgement Day when Skynet goes live in the year 2017***

Autonomous Artificial Intelligence will be the next matrix environment to follow

Objectives: 100% control of the human mind, obliterate revolts with excessive force

> ***The human WILL negates control, the main reason the tools of the matrix in 1984 will have to be re-implemented***

March 1st 2016 an article of continuance to open our eyes even further. Scientists discover how to 'upload knowledge to your brain'

By Mark Molloy

Feeding knowledge directly into your brain, just like in sci-fi classic The Matrix, could soon take as much effort as falling asleep, scientists believe. Researchers claim to have developed a simulator which can feed information directly into a person's brain and teach them new skills in a shorter amount of time, comparing it to "life imitating art".

They believe it could be the first steps in developing advanced software that will make Matrix-style instant learning a reality.

In the neo-noir sci-fi classic, protagonist Neo is able to learn kung fu in seconds after the martial art is 'uploaded' straight to his brain.

Researchers from HRL Laboratories, based in California, say they have found a way to amplify learning, only on a much smaller scale than seen in the Hollywood film.

They studied the electric signals in the brain of a trained pilot and then fed the data into novice subjects as they learned to pilot an aeroplane in a realistic flight simulator.

The study, published in the journal Frontiers in Human Neuroscience, found that subjects who received brain stimulation via electrode-embedded head caps improved their piloting abilities and learnt the task 33 per cent better than a placebo group.

Our system is one of the first of its kind. It's a brain stimulation system," explained Dr Matthew Phillips.

"It sounds kind of sci-fi, but there's large scientific basis for the development of our system.

"The specific task we were looking at was piloting an aircraft, which requires a synergy of both cognitive and motor performance.

"When you learn something, your brain physically changes. Connections are made and strengthened in a process called neuro-plasticity.

"It turns out that certain functions of the brain, like speech and memory, are located in very specific regions of the brain, about the size of your pinky."

Dr Matthews believes that brain stimulation could eventually be implemented for tasks like learning to drive, exam preparation and language learning

"What our system does is it actually targets those changes to specific regions of the brain as you learn," he added.

The method itself is actually quite old. In fact, the ancient Egyptians 4000 years ago used electric fish to stimulate and reduce pain.

"Even Ben Franklin applied currents to his head, but the rigorous, scientific investigation of these methods started in the early 2000s and we're building on that research to target and personalise a stimulation in the most effective way possible.

"Your brain is going to be very different to my brain when we perform a task. What we found is … brain stimulation seems to be particularly effective at actually improving learning."

Which pill are you going to absorb the red or the blue

As perception of the matrix pill at certain times of peaceful revolt tend to be altered without reflection, we're being assured in a future not far from our grasp that the equality of perception will dominate our thoughts, dismissing our will to choose the ***matrix pill***

Founding Fathers

John Adams, **Benjamin Franklin**, **Alexander Hamilton**, John Jay, **Thomas Jefferson**, **James Madison**, and **George Washington**.

The magnanimous, & magnificent seven: ***Our Founding Fathers may be esteemed for getting the United States of America started, but they were still regular people, with all-too-human quirks, personality flaws, and family issues. One was too shy to talk to a crush (or just about anyone else), another hated his post-independence job, and one honored gentleman occasionally exploded into paroxysms of rage. The Founding Fathers: They're just like us!***

Philadelphia September 17, 1787, a historical calendar day when the magnificent seven along with

Thirty one delegates signed the United States Constitution.

Beyond clever; {Unifying A Diverse People} sound familiar. The primary aim of the Constitution was to create a strong elected government, directly responsive to the will of the people. Drafted by fifty five delegates under severe urgency and tension to preserve peace, & ? lets not deny the fact, these are politicians (liberating the magnificent seven from title) conserving position and guaranteeing future prosperity for All.

Two hundred twenty nine years and these brilliant arrangement of words are able to continue transmitting the power bestowed them since drafted.

Unfortunately, the essence of the Constitution cannot be summoned upon like a Jeannie in a bottle, to exercise its main directive, the will of the people. The authority and empowerment is passed onto our elected officials, but more often than imaginable it seems the Directive is lost in translation.

Broken promises are not lies, they are a mere misunderstanding, expecting the hybrid word yeno to be added to the dictionary resolving the confusion.

A maverick approach to limit the amount of money donated by any institution or person in order to avoid the pitfall of a purchased election.

Politicos the cat leaped out of the hat, stop trying to impose a chimeric all is fine environment, instead of dissolving the fool's paradise we live in with the unvarnished truth

Your Genius Is Glowing

Relentlessly trying to stamp surname in the history books
blurred your walk of life

Quasi bipartisanship is the consequence of your search to
etch your laurels upon us

Enervated are the people of our diverse cultural nation after
every laurel's hardship is forced upon them

As they tirade against your inoculations you eschew their
words with florid verbose

Avoiding bedlam by transiently allaying their fears of
supplementary pecuniary oppression

To Serve radically in times of great distress will cause a
global disturbance of 9.0 magnitude on the Richter scale

Adequate needed solutions to stop kicking the osmium can
down to the next generation will be fiercely contested by
everyone

Then who are we but a mere representation of the
generations before us

Who have left us with the responsibility of curing all their
miscalculations

A great onus which we decide to leave as inheritance to our
children because we lack courage to mend today for a better
life to come tomorrow

Are Governments Their Children's Godfather & Vice Versa

A duel between Aron Burr and Alexander Hamilton which began at dawn July 11, 1804 in Weehawken, New Jersey ended Hamilton's life in his late 40s. Leaving behind his wife Eliza and children with limited resources to continue forward.

Luckily his dignity was rescued with an $80,000.00 donation from political friends which was divulged one hundred thirty three years later in 1937.

"I came here to tell you the truth, the good, the bad and the ugly."

"I am here to accept responsibility for that which I did.
I will not accept responsibility for that which I did not do."
"I'm trusting in the Lord and a good lawyer."
Renowned quotes from Oliver North, remember the Reagan years and the Iran-Contra scandal, Oliver North was convicted of selling arms to rebels to be later cleared of all charges, he never implicated the president.

A shocking abuse of presidential power in January 2001, his last day in power, Bill Clinton issued a presidential pardon to fugitive Marc Rich, congress blocked the pardon.

To continue evidence would require too many zerabytes of data, hopefully this sliver of information that leap generations is suffice to convince.

The Wrath Of The Law

For whom shall they apply, we the people are unsure

Secrets held in the dark till anger fades and the people reconcile while others never see the light

Evidence enhances or retrogresses, your name shall decide

Maneuvering perception swaying the court's hammer to convict or ***EVICT***

Evidence enhances or retrogresses, your fingerprints shall decide

Maneuvering perception swaying the court's hammer to evict or ***CONVICT***

Evidence enhances or retrogresses, your DNA shall decide

Maneuvering perception swaying the court's hammer to ***GUARANTEE CONVICTION***

Your honor is it the truth we seek in the name of justice
or is it a sacrifice we seek to preserve justice before the three tier pyramid

Impeachment Of Negatives

Vulnerability towards godawful comportment can ultimately culminate in the fatal severance of the will

In defense for our actions or inaction we are accustomed to prefabricated dialogue, to soothe repugnance towards ourselves

Once acclimated to consistently act injudiciously, the context of virtuous & maleficent, have nil variance

Counterbalancing the human scale, while avoiding conviction on the two extremes is not a lucid everyday living task, nevertheless a mindset focused on The Golden Rule, is a positive beginning to a decent honorable foundation

Inflation-Deflation Fast Forward

Simple in theory but ambiguously distorted by economic indicators

2008 the weight of ten items would equal 266oz for a total of x price

2016 the weight of the exact ten items equal 232oz for a total of x price

Consumer Price Index, a flexible basket of goods that once a product becomes too expensive in accordance with their definition is replaced with a lessor value product altering the end result of your budget

Economic indicators suggest with concrete stats that the global economy is in a deflationary cycle

The seal of secrecy as to why, how and who creates these economic numbers is inconclusive to say the least

September 08, 2016 the US Federal Reserve, Bank Of Japan, ECB, and England have so far flooded the world with $9,000,000,000,000.00 of newly printed money and counting

The question and answer to the distortion of our economic indicators lies in who is benefiting the most from the massive creation of wealth

A rogue global alliance so indeterminably debauched with no restraint or discouragement in sight, because they will never be touched by the Penal Institution.

Lost In Congressional Lingua Franca

Experiencing bewilderment from our political home is by no
means accidental

Conveying to their citizens what they mean, but by no means
promulgate true intentions

The polarization of language used by our Statesmen changes
in accordance with the distress level needed to accomplish
their chef-d'oeuvre

Setbacks are acknowledged generations following

Acknowledged by virtue of the price tag becoming their onus

Exceptionally skilled at creating divergence of their true
promulgation we will forever dwindle into their abyss

Lost In Lover's Lanes

As there are eight lanes in sight of mind, at times we're not sure of our loss

As there are eight lanes indulging our heart, at times we're not sure of our gain

Eros, a time of readiness to extract lust from all the beautiful flowers

Philia's degree of certainty involves dismissing your needs for your family and at times your friends

Storge rises from shared interest among family and friends centered in a circle of selfishness

Ah Ludus, hunting season for the male youth on those beautiful summer nights

Mania directs the injured mind involved to a state of obsessive behavior causing mental and sometimes physical abuse to the innocent

Pragma, only relished if you have discovered how to endure the test of time, love of the minds

Philautia is a lone journeying through the lanes before you are able to offer them to others

Agape is a universal mental peacefulness that allows you to love societies and nature with aught egocentricity

Lost a key to open feelings utilized in my aesthetic years of love, what am I missing?

Lost a twin latchkey for loving thyself and thyself only, why am I so lonely?

Found a key to share all my significance with their interests, why am I not happy?

Found a key to only temporarily ignite my feelings of love, who or what am I?

Lost a key which forever has sterilized my capacity to bequeath myself to love, why me?

Found a twin latchkey because I'm patient with true love, why am I so happy?

Never lost a key, progression of the journey through the lanes has empowered me to love as I love myself, why am I so unconditional?

Found the combination to love that ignores hatred and lives within our souls why am I feeling so sublime?

To question what we have lost is not by accident or coincidence, as love is very perplexing, with an abundance of significance to engage our heart's palpitations

To question what we have gained is not by realization or incident, as love is a societal need, obscuring the mind with thy heart's feelings even when it's camouflaged

Albeit it's intrinsic influence at times causes animated mental and physical distress, and in lieu of the prize to be procured from the love within the gem; lest not despair to avert it's yearning, instead release the gates of your heart and hope to discover the ultimate triumph from it's value:

!! A TREASURE TROVE OF PASSION!!

Morality Impact

Morality, the Judge Dredd to discipline people against
all vices that inflict psychological & physical abuse onto
themselves and others

Did Judge Dredd board the Jules Verne Train to never return
or was he ever really within reach?

Morality at times when situational ethics calls upon it for a
dire decision or direction stretches its boundaries becoming
more taut to accommodate the course of action

What we have today is infinite moral elasticity with
happiness on the drivers' seat as an integral justification,
triggering the calibration & direction of the moral compass

A mournful state of affair creating a vulgar & shameless
environment we call home

George Washington, "No generation has the right to contract debts greater than can be paid off during the course of its own existence."

Article 10 Clause 1 Of Our Constitution:

No State shall enter into any Treaty, Alliance, or Confederation; grant Letters of Marque and Reprisal; coin Money; emit Bills of Credit; make any Thing but gold and silver Coin a Tender in Payment of Debts; pass any Bill of Attainder, ex post facto Law, or Law impairing the Obligation of **Contracts, or grant any Title of Nobility.**

Henry Ford famously said, *"It is well enough that people of the nation do not understand our banking and monetary system, for if they did, I believe there would be a revolution before tomorrow morning."*

Sir Josiah Stamps: Director of the Bank Of England 1928-1940

.

"Banking was conceived in iniquity and was born in sin. The Bankers own the earth. Take it away from them, but leave them the power to create deposits,and with the flick of the pen they will create enough deposits to buy it back again. However, take it away from them, and all the great fortunes like mine will disappear and they ought to disappear, for this would be a happier and better world

**to live in. But, if you wish to remain the slaves of Bankers and pay the cost of your own slavery,
let them continue to create deposits."**

1913, the birth of an institution (The Federal Reserve), so supreme it molds every aspect of our lives, from our daily plates to the threads we wear.

Lest not forget a fact of this year, a fishy accident occurred the Federal income tax was mothered by the Federal Reserve to breast feed us till retirement and beyond.

2008 the year you were at the brink of recognition but wiggled from under like a worm avoiding capture, for the taxpayer will be forevermore indebted for your lack of courage to expose yourself.

Have the pronounced adjustments defended 2008 from reoccurring, you elect a victor.

Roberto Duran vs Davey Moore, Luis Resto vs Billy Collins Jr, Muhammad Ali vs Joe Frazier, Barry McGuigan vs Steve Cruz, Marvin Hagler vs Thomas Hearns, Dennis Andries vs Jeff Harding, & Joe Calzaghe vs Chris Eubank.

The seven most brutal boxing fights in the history of this gaudy sport is a morsel of what will be the results of the next merciless round against the clout champion Who Are You ***and it's opponent, a slayed lamb*** Taxpayer.

Who Are You?

Afraid of cross referencing on behalf of all your fallible
credentials transmitting financial chaos in every door step
exonerating yours truly

Valid purpose to exist eludes us while accepting a belief that

your subsistence is beneficial or face dire financial consequences

The art of deception, prominent in your disguise, sending Lehman

Brothers to the slaughter house, diverting showtime from real

intent to save thyself at the cost of butchering the masses

A syndicate bearing witness to The Three Musketeers motto

Unus pro omnibus, omnes pro uno, stay compliant for all and the

fat lady will never sing The End Is Near by Rulebreaker

Parlaying Ignorance

Rare to witness an event where the unnatural occurs,
gallantry dis-avowing egocentricity and rivalry

To set aside enmity and coadunate forces on behalf of all
others is meritable & beyond pardon

Verity of the event is not an issue, as all others are
perpetually consign to oblivion

If realism is not embodied in the message, it will be
manufactured allaying all others burden of a mix up
mystification

Once assurances are addressed, the doters will gladly offer
all their support either secretly to both sides or publicly to
one side

The method is a series of actions to attain and conclude
results

The subjects is a series of speeches to attain and conclude
results

Once results are confirmed the beneficiaries are known
through a suspended reality, never lapsing from illusion

Plausible Paradox

The dark occult year and all are directed toward the polygraph purpose {Humane Thermostat} test in which a human's value added merits will be reckoned before they are adept to take flight to Mars.

From beginning to end our empty carapace will be exposed to innumerable menus of options on how we acquire success

The journey you elect is structured upon your definition of success, a winner definition without accountability leads to the eradication of all that envelops you, near your end, a belated recognition that you have been eradicating yourself thusly for success, your visa to flight is denied

The ultimate question to the ultimate test, why did you choose to become who you are has zero {0} earthly value, your answer must be factual or the test will deny you the misuse of words, factual words, preconditioned to reflect spiritual stature

Procuring a Healthy Elan Vital

As with our nourishing of our mortal elements is cardinal in order to shield it from natural maladies

Lets ruminate the nourishment of our uttermost remarkable element

A unique malady is of grave concern, the propinquity
of sanity to insanity is irrelevant as long as its fortitude
stalemates the befitting side

Victual this crucial element with knowledge that accentuates what makes us human

Explicit knowledge can be captured in words and your ability to retain them

Tacit knowledge calls forth judgment, emotions, and
complexities that is absorbed only through experience,
making the abecedarians better humans

Ceaseless nourishment through knowledge is de rigueur for societies to arise within themselves

Psychedelic mushrooms can do more than make you see the world in kaleidoscope. Research suggests they may have permanent, positive effects on the human brain.

In fact, a mind-altering compound found in some 200 species of mushroom is already being explored as a potential treatment for depression and anxiety. People who consume these mushrooms, after "trips" that can be a bit scary and unpleasant, report feeling more optimistic, less self-centered, and even happier for months after the fact.

But why do these trips change the way people see the world? According to a study published today in *Human Brain Mapping*, the mushroom compounds could be unlocking brain states usually only experienced when we dream, changes in activity that could help unlock permanent shifts in perspective.

The study examined brain activity in those who'd received injections of psilocybin, which gives "shrooms" their psychedelic punch. Despite a long history of mushroom use in spiritual practice, scientists have only recently begun to examine the brain activity of those using the compound, and this is the first study to attempt to relate the behavioral effects to biological changes.

After injections, the 15 participants were found to have increased brain function in areas associated with emotion and memory. The effect was strikingly similar to a brain in dream sleep, according to Dr. Robin Carhart-Harris, a post-doctoral researcher in neuropsychopharmacology at Imperial College London and co-author of the study.

"You're seeing these areas getting louder, and more active," he said. "It's like someone's turned up the volume there, in these regions that are considered part of an emotional system in the brain. When you look at a brain during dream sleep, you see the same hyperactive emotion centers."

In fact, administration of the drug just before or during sleep seemed to promote higher activity levels during Rapid Eye Movement sleep, when dreams occur. An intriguing finding, Carhart-Harris says, given that people tend to describe their experience on psychedelic drugs as being like "a waking dream." It seems that the brain may literally be slipping into unconscious patterns while the user is awake.

Conversely, the subjects of the study had decreased activity in other parts of the brain—areas associated with high level cognition. "These are the most recent parts of our brain, in an evolutionary sense," Carhart-Harris said. "And we see them getting quieter and less organized."

This dampening of one area and amplification of another could explain the "mind-broadening" sensation of psychedelic drugs, he said. Unlike most recreational drugs, psychotropic mushrooms and LSD don't provide a pleasant, hedonistic reward when they're consumed. Instead, users take them very occasionally, chasing the strange neurological effects instead of any sort of high.

"Except for some naïve users who go looking for a good time…which, by the way, is not how it plays out," Carhart-Harris said, "you see people taking them to experience some kind of mental exploration, and to try to understand themselves."

Our firm sense of self—the habits and experiences that we find integral to our personality—is quieted by these trips. Carhart-Harris believes that the drugs may unlock emotion while "basically killing the ego," allowing users to be less narrow-minded and let go of negative outlooks.

It's still not clear why such effects can have more profound long-term effects on the brain than our nightly dreams. But Carhart-Harris hopes to see more of these compounds in modern medicine. "The way we treat psychological illnesses now is to dampen things," he said. "We dampen anxiety, dampen ones emotional range in the hope of curing depression, taking the sting out of what one feels."

But some patients seem to benefit from having their emotions "unlocked" instead. "It would really suit the style of psychotherapy where we engage in a patient's history and hang-ups," Carhart-Harris said. "Instead of putting a bandage over the exposed wound, we'd be essentially loosening their minds—promoting a permanent change in outlook."

The Prognosis – The Cure Outlier Possibilities

Lest not concern over mere imperfections with harmless minuscule outcomes

To ruminate on those who will hoard power without regard for the number of human sacrifice

Possibilities abound in the unlocking of the human brain, at it's rudimentary stages, light bulbs of hope are flashing, signaling an imaginable cure

Lest not despair to think about it's ethical or non ethical argument until you have read these names that follow Kim Jong II, Mobutu Sese Seko, Francois Duvalier, Saparmurat Niyazov, Francisco Macias Nguema, YahJa Jammeh, Muammar Qaddafi, Idi Amin, Rafael Trujillo, Nicolae Ceausescu, the top ten insane dictators and many more not mentioned with an unknown number of human casualties

Unscrupulous casualties for the sake of power, the prognosis is in dire distress of a cure

Their actions indoctrinates a permanent preconception that mercy, and repenting are feelings of an inferior leader

Love others, other than thyself is not an option for these non compos mentis.

Reticent Affiliate Or Foe To Destiny

Temporal length of events in every juncture of our lives is our
rival-ally or in unison hinging on our psyche and spirit

A priceless irreplaceable intangible asset of monumental
universal value without jurisdiction or ownership

It disciplines every facet of all existing beings regardless of your
ecological, financial, strength, or metronymic status

Albeit it's not possible to grasp and control, it's freely
accessible to all, and if managed appropriately, it will be your
tenacious ally indeed

If managed in an undisciplined chaotic behavior, it will be
your cataclysmic rival naturally

If not managed at all, a labyrinth without an outlet or
significance prevails

The distinction between living out your life and living your
life disrupting the complacency of our existing status

El Suspiro De La Juventud

The sigh of youth are the genuine Golden Years of all humans expressed through beauty, virility, and an insatiable desire for knowledge of the veiled adulthood interactions

Time will mature us from our aesthetic phase into a complacency where we matter less for our new arrivals to transfer our names

Time once again will hopefully convert us into wise men to deliver guidance to the ones we once were, our beloved youths

Before you negate your maturity remember your denial is virulent as Time has no compassion and is uncompromising to all

Tariff Addictus Aficionado

How shrewd are you to envision a tax that will voluntarily donate to the treasury

Enthusiastic and overjoyed to donate forming extensive long lines asking to be stripped of their legal tender

The promise of investing in the future of our offspring is a heinous excuse to catapult revenue to the stratosphere

The pot of gold is filled, fleeced leaving snippets, refilled, fleeced leaving snippets

The process continues until the snippets are dispersed out of pity

For those Reluctant to participate on the line to glory, there is a line for everyone

A line formed once a year and obviously for your hearts content you do it for your offspring

Fleecing the sheep has always been top priority, the coiffures change structures but not their essence

Anger and revolt were top priority as evidenced December 16, 1773, today eagerness to be fleeced and a glass of champagne to celebrate is the norm

The Masks Hidden Under The 21 Facial Expressions

To entertain ourselves by arousing or ascertain a desired behavior from another we show the power of facial empathy

To gain property from another either for fun or utility we show the power of facial necessity

The masks intentions on the other hand are at times concealed under our facade

Concealed under the circumstance the other is getting the short end of the stick

Despair-not to inform the masks that his accolades and great skills at achieving distorted behavior of another upon his whimsical request is best utilized in Hollywood

Virtual Reciprocal Communication

Condolences to yesteryear's proper form of a one to one
tete-a-tete

Somatic ocular blindness is the fashionable form of our
bygone days of social tea time

Virtual transmission reflecting our thoughts and feelings
can never compare with resonating words from someone's
persona

Envision a 3D image of a man or a woman exacerbating your
urge for the irreplaceable human touch

Then why move in progression instead of regression
involving human interaction?

Inquisitiveness will excite our minds until eventually
devastate our identity of humanity, kindness, mercy, and
sympathy

Unraveling Of A Weasel

Shrewd to cloak and re-cloak at any beacon of impartance

His proclaimed identity is one of stature and stringent caliber of virtues

To chaperon all his one friends at the cost of marring all who cross his path

His repartee are profoundly skewed towards dishonesty and slightly skewed towards truthfulness

As confusion sets in, his inability to record a transcript of all that has been spoken will eventually accelerate his charade en route to a revelation of his verisimilitude

One Soul, One Palace, One Conscious

Yearning for him, arrival of my Prince to capture my heart's dream, awakening in his arms

Yearning for her acceptance to be my Queen, our love carried by the wind enlivening colors of every rainbow, sprouting all flowers in the garden, harmonic melody dispersed by every stroke of the wind

A gentleman's bait and lady's capture indeed, the love is authentic and by no means a fairy tale, longevity is the obstacle turned fable

Their hearts transformed into one as he, as she unhinged their love by laying aside each one's individualism and selfishness, denouement of the greatest love possible

We wish for it, few are fortunate to experience it, but once we have it, we live the rest of our lives challenging it, thus disallowing growth of its wonder

The Offshoot Of Repetitive Episodes

Launched after nascence, it's the first encounter with the construct of your personality

Your purlieu, a pattern of colors, people, travel, human touch, readings, and feeding; nurturing your perception

A private library visited without awareness, it's a recollection of your development

The desire to repent at times of dishonor, it's a reminder that this is not who you are

The architect responsible for building your character are all the installments in your library, allowing you to seek the correct path in accordance with your noble compass

As guardians, our assignment is eternal and challenging, but the glory to see them develop into an individual greater than us is our most significant satisfying reward

Conceding to defer guidance should not be an option of practice, as they are allowed to fail us, but we have no excuses to fail them

Moral Soldiers With Unyielding Courage

After reading Jim Henrys' fact set research report "How the Kleptocrats' $12 Trillion Heist Helps Keep Most Of the World Impoverished" by David Cay Johnston and audibly absorbing the Monologue "Ellos" from Roberto Mtz over and over

The resistance encasing my despair, that was denying me to write with disregard for whom would feel prosecuted has been attenuated

My tears have fallen inside my circle of confidence renouncing the laughter of the blue blooded establishment

I'm a vigorous believer in love, optimism, the virtues, good sense, and the truth in which it will never introduce a second opportunity, only lies need second chances

The human family will always be in some kind of circumstantial difficulty, but division between the establishment and the commoners magnifies the uncontrollable level of corruption ensuing a total disruption of our values

A false invisible embrace from them assuring us that all is well is just their urgency for us to accept the inherited system as it is

The formidable power they obtain did not create or changed the color of blood flowing through their veins or in any way corrupt them, it wholly immensely enhanced their corrupted heart and essence from within

To show weakness when our heart senses immoral actions and lack the courage to respond in proper principle, hence we are becoming just like them

A sheath of snake venom embodied in every planck length of their bodies and souls, wistfully this is what they are

The journey to forestalling the cancer of corruption encircling us starts with you, spreading one good action at a time, a contagion we need to transmit throughout our human family and our home Earth

Deliquescing Away Correlation Comparisons

To observe knowing all partiality of thy neighbors without
knowing art thou's own, is a fragmented thought

A clear and precise compilation of data will lead critical
thinking to separate facts from the recognition of
assumptions

It's an impasse idea to consider a mind neutral to all
information that's forthcoming, hence stepping outside
conventional wisdom is key for finding new solutions and to
pen objective beliefs and values

Nonce and impending input collection, evaluated
with contemporary wisdom, setting aside instinctive
predispositions would output the fairest of all interpretations

If judging within these boundaries is viable, the out-crying
for justice in detriment of thy neighbor will markedly abate

Besides, out-crying is freely dispersed and entertaining,
however it's very time consuming and since time is money,
donating, auctioning, and or purchase of sobbing is nil in a
prejudicial landscape

Bred To The Bone Biases

A question was asked, a comment was voiced, an article was scanned, a controversial topic was aired, the rebuttal was terrifying

A question was asked, a comment was voiced, an article was scanned, a controversial topic was aired, the rebuttal was valid

A question was asked, a comment was voiced, an article was scanned, a controversial topic was aired, the rebuttal was neutral

A question was asked, a comment was voiced, an article was scanned, a controversial topic was aired, the rebuttal was objective until facts of study were scrutinized

Mind boggling to hear yourself after a rewind of your shoot first and ask questions later rebuttal, at times wounding profoundly everyone known and unknown including your loved ones

As intellectual and precise is your argument, Availability Cascade will dictate the swing of the pendulum, be careful not to lose yourself

A good stance without any distribution of pain

The most judicious form of approach as long as iron clad subjectivity doesn't interfere with your intellect allowing for System Justification

Actualism Awareness

Few ever experience the possibility that they are incapable of
acknowledging altruistic self awareness

Evidenced in the inability to be genuinely kind and have
courage of acceptance of oneself and others as we're too
laissez faire to conduct introspection of our integrity

We care for the safety of our transport by checking its'
integrity to keep us from hazardous travel

We tirade about others as an everyday exercise of
intelligence, creating an accepted vituperative environment

Lets reflect on our image, what can we recognize,
ARE WE BETTER THAN OUR PAST?
CAN WE BE BETTER IN THE FUTURE?
ARE WE BETTER THAN WE EVER THOUGHT?

The Mirror Of Denial

The thick cloud upon the mirror, discovery is a planck away

Divergence of thought is of daily task from a child of five to
your final day

The day your fear is no longer deliquescing away the truth

Your parents are of no consequence to whom you are,
juxtaposing development retired your own thoughts

Infinitely accepting social continuity to digest sanity as the
only conclusion

The wrath of nature, the glorious carnage of war, granting
thy neighbor a free pass of love, fortifying the barricades of
our accommodated fear

A spurious reality our dualistic existence must adhere, or
face insanity encircling the sphere

One life contends its fragility to oppose denial and its lies,
the other afraid of dishonor to be judged and forced towards
insufferable seclusion

Tomorrow at sunrise the thick cloud upon the mirror
renewed, the denial and its lies forevermore endure

The Grand Bubba Effect

Dignifying an anti humility stance by proclaiming an
illustrious presence of him or herself leads to an ultra
pretentious persona

In consequence his or her ears automatically filter out all that
matters to another

Eyes will construct a virtual tunnel vision, perception of
reality only seen through a backwards view of a telescope

Data is processed through a prescribed set of rules, words
to cause insensitivity are exiled to the back door, words of
praise are kept in a repetitive loop until renewed

Love, self indulged hearts without space for another

These exoteric beings are living among us and are invisible
to those who pander them to glory

Distinguishable by asking yourself who is the uttermost
contemptible and condescending in the room

The Complexity Of Electing A Democratic Servant

Surrender before your guilt, after fornicating your honor in defense of your ego

Never again will you be the same, not because of what they think of you, but because of what you think of yourself

You neglected the actions of a decent man or woman, and betrayed his or her dignity for satisfaction of your ascetic narcissism

Everyone deserves a free pass for first time noncompliance, the dilemma is of continuity to corrupt your soul, devaluing the principles of your sworn oath

If defiance to whom you serve arouses your intellect, shown in vain when you suppress protest, thence serving only yourself and colleagues

Under an unscrupulous tenure, you ask us to trust your demeanor, but how can we trust a mountebank with a reckless sense of morality, we don’t, but choose to extend his(her) position because he(she) is the most remarkably curtailed villain

Printed in the United States
By Bookmasters